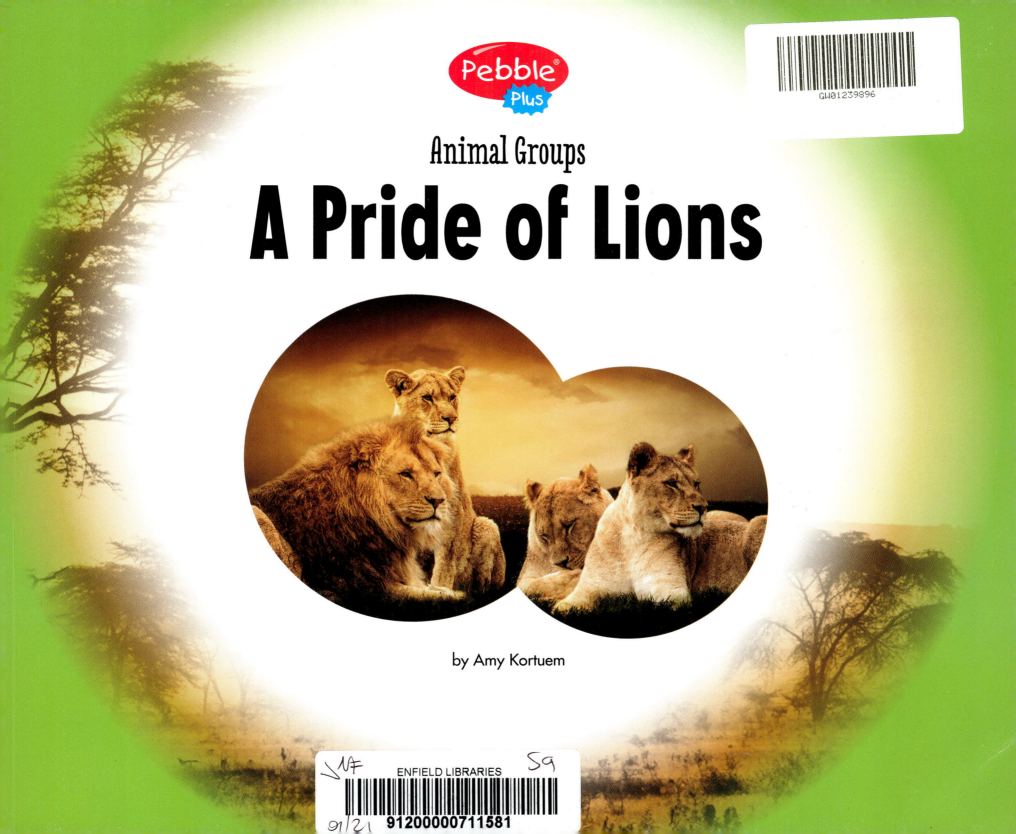

Pebble® Plus

Animal Groups

A Pride of Lions

by Amy Kortuem

Raintree is an imprint of Capstone Global Library Limited, a company
incorporated in England and Wales having its registered office at 264 Banbury
Road, Oxford, OX2 7DY – Registered company number: 6695582

www.raintree.co.uk
myorders@raintree.co.uk

Edited by Abby Colich
Designed by Tracy McCabe
Original illustrations © Capstone Global Library Limited 2020
Picture research by Eric Gohl
Production by Kathy McColley
Originated by Capstone Global Library Ltd
Printed and bound in India

978 1 4747 8530 3 (hardback)
978 1 4747 8536 5 (paperback)

British Library Cataloguing in Publication Data
A full catalogue record for this book is available from the British Library.

Acknowledgements
We would like to thank the following for permission to reproduce
photographs: Alamy: AfriPics.com, 15; iStockphoto: Brett Durrant, 7, jez_
bennett, 17, mantaphoto, 11, Marie Holding, back cover (right), 21, pchoui, 5,
Serge_Vero, back cover (bottom), 19; Newscom: ZUMA Press/Ingo Gerlach, 13;
Shutterstock: Galyna Andrushko, background, ichywong, 9, STANZI, cover, 1

Every effort has been made to contact copyright holders of material reproduced
in this book. Any omissions will be rectified in subsequent printings if notice is
given to the publisher.

All the internet addresses (URLs) given in this book were valid at the time
of going to press. However, due to the dynamic nature of the internet, some
addresses may have changed, or sites may have changed or ceased to exist
since publication. While the author and publisher regret any inconvenience this
may cause readers, no responsibility for any such changes can be accepted by
either the author or the publisher.

Contents

What is a pride?

It is hot in Africa.
Tall grasses wave. What is
hiding? It's a pride of lions!
Their fur matches the colour
of the grass.

About 15 to 40 lions live together in a group. The group is called a pride. Most are females and cubs. Up to three adult males live with them.

A pride lives and hunts in the same area. This is called a territory. Males protect this area. Females hunt there. Cubs play and learn to hunt.

Lion cubs grow

It's time to give birth!
The female leaves the pride.
She hides in a den. She has
two or three cubs. They can leave
the den after five weeks.

Female cubs stay with the pride. Males leave the pride when they are around two years old. They look for a new territory. Some try to join another pride. They fight the pride's males for a place.

On the hunt

Lions eat other large mammals. Females hunt together. They watch and listen for prey. They sneak up on the prey to get close.

Females run fast towards prey. Their legs are strong. Big paws catch the prey. The lions tear the meat with sharp teeth. Males eat first. Females and cubs eat last.

Lion talk

Roar! Lions roar to find each other. They also roar when danger is near. They show their sharp teeth and claws too. They scare away lions from other prides.

Lions make other sounds. They growl when angry or nervous. Lions may swat or bite at others. This shows they are not happy. They huff and purr when relaxed.

Glossary

cub young lion

den place where a wild animal may live

huff blow in short gusts

mammal warm-blooded animal that breathes air, has fur and feeds milk to its young

prey animal hunted by another animal for food

swat hit quickly

territory land on which an animal grazes or hunts for food and cares for its young

Find out more

Books

Big Cats (DKfindout!), DK (DK Children, 2019)

Lion: Killer King of the Plains (Top of the Food Chain), Louise Spilsbury (Raintree, 2019)

Lion vs Tiger (Animal Rivals), Isabel Thomas (Raintree, 2018)

Websites

www.bbc.co.uk/programmes/p018yxrr
More facts about lions.

www.dkfindout.com/uk/animals-and-nature/cats/lion
Find out more about lions and listen to a lion roar!

Comprehension questions

1. What do lions in a pride do together?
2. What is a territory?
3. Why do lions roar?

Index